Why Nazism and White Racism Suck

And Do Nothing But Empower Leftists And Hurt The White Race

Wyatt Kaldenberg

1

ISBN-10: 146644147X

ISBN-13: 978-1466441477

Other Books by Wyatt Kaldenberg

Odinism for Beginners: An Introduction to the Odinic Heathen Religion

Odinism: The Religion of Our Germanic Ancestors In the Modern World: Essays on the Heathen Revival and the Return of the Age of the Gods

Perceived Heathenism & Odinic Prayer: A Book of Heathen Prayer and Direct Contact with Our Living Gods

Odinism In The Age of Man: The Dark Age before the return of our Gods

Odinism: Inside the Belly of the Beast: Essays on Heathenism inside The New World Order

A Heathen Family Devotional: Odinism Begins at Home

The Little Book of Heathen Prayers for Heathen Kids: A Collection of Odinic Prayers for Children

ALSO: I make a reprint of the famous 1800s fantasy novel, The Oera Linda Book, as well as an Anthology of Early Norse & Germanic Neo-Pagans: The Early Years of Asatru & Odinism

Table of Contents

Chapter One

Nazism and Racism Hurts the White Race

Young racist, I am not going to put you down for being involved in the racist movement. I totally understand it. I know how fucked up this system is. I know this system has nothing to offer the average White working class person. Indeed, I was involved in the movement for a little over a decade. I am not anti-White at all. I am very pro-White. I am against the movement because it misleads our people. The racist movement and National Socialism address real problems our people face. Unfortunately, they cloud up these issues with so much hate and foolishness that they drive our people away from supporting matters which they should and would support if not for the god-damned movement. It makes you wonder who is really behind the racist movement.

Rich Whites live like medieval kings. Working-class Whites are not so blessed.

Non-Whites are treated as the "Golden Children" and "The Eternal Victims." White working-class people and the White poor are seen as "Privileged" and "The Oppressor of the World", while at the same time we are "stupid, worthless poor White trash." The White male is just as demonized today under liberal democracy as the Jews were demonized in America and in Germany during the 1920s.

If Henry Ford were alive today, he would write a book called the International White Male. I am waiting for Hollywood to make a remake of the Eternal Jew, but this time call it the Eternal White Man.

It's easy to hate this system. This system deserves to be hated. I hate this system, too. It may not be this year or even this century, but one day this system will collapse, and when that day comes, it will be the greatest day in Western history.

I know this, and you know this. However, I

Why Nazism and White Racism Suck

am not writing this to tell you how screwed up the system is. What I am about to tell you is why you should not join the White racist movement, and if you are already a member, why you should drop out.

I am aiming this booklet at young people because I feel most older people in the movement are a lost cause.

I am not writing this from an anti-White point of view because I don't hate the White race. I am writing this from the viewpoint that the White racist movement does nothing but hurt our White race and plays into the hands of the people who hate us.

I will not make this a long book, because of two reasons: Primarily, I want this to be a booklet that folks can cheaply and easily hand out to young people in the movement. Secondly, it will be hard to get people in the racist cause to read even a small booklet that criticizes the movement, and impossible to get them to read a larger book.

Yes, the racist movement addresses real problems, but it goes about it the wrong way.

The number one complaint I have heard people use for leaving the so-called movement is it does nothing but turn good White people off, and it enriches, both politically and financially, anyone who fights "hate." There is an entire industry that has grown around fighting the poor White trash in the "hate movement." They collect money from mainly rich liberals who view poor Whites as green toothed, Bible thumping Klansmen living in trailer parks and selling crystal meth. The rich Whites hate poor Whites and see them as just pale-skinned Negroes, who they can never win any Politically-Correct brownie points by supporting. They donate large amounts of money to the "anti-hate" industry in hopes that it will wipe the poor Whites off the face of the earth. The White racist movement feeds into this stereotype the affluent liberals have of the White working-class. Racists cause liberals to give money to non-profit groups that make fortunes spreading negative stereotypes about poor Whites and White Southerners. It is tax deductible in addition to being Politically Correct.

This is a "win-win" for the liberals.

Many folks on the Left, or perhaps they are merely milking the Left, have found that "fighting hate" is the ultimate "cash cow."

Why Nazism and White Racism Suck

Recently, the former publisher of the Icelandic Arisk Upprisa (Aryan Uprising) journal told me, "If I were to go back in time and do it all over again I would not come near the N.S. stuff. The N.S. stuff puts people off, or they simply did not get it. Even though a lot of people were against immigration and multi-culturism, the whole Hitler thing kept them away. And the funny thing is nobody talks about Arisk Upprisa anymore except left wing journalists moaning about Neo-Nazism." It seems no one is interested in joining movements that idolize mass murderers, except for the middle and upper class university students who join left-wing groups that cherish mass murderers like Lenin, Trotsky, Stalin, Mao, Pol Pot, Che, Castro, and the others. Working-class White folks just aren't into psychotic killers like the rich college-educated liberals are.

I know National Socialism seems like an attractive alternative to liberal Democracy.

Liberal democracy is one of the greatest lies in human history. Democracy promises to empower the people, but there has never been even a brief second in history where democracy empowered the people. Actually, how can the people ever rule anything? Are the people a great monolith? Are they a single person with a single mind? If not, how could they ever rule?

Democracy is like having the people drive a single car at the same time. It's impossible. The people control nothing under democracy. Democracy is controlled by small groups of bickering demagogues, lobbyists, and special-interest groups all backed up by money.

If you don't have money, democracy doesn't give a fuck about you, except around election time when they so graciously allow the average boob to pick between system-candidate: A, B, or C. And, if on that rare occasion a non-system candidate does get heard by the people, the system will do every it can to marginalize, defame, and destroy that maverick candidate.

I am in my 50s and in just half a century, I have seen this happen in every democracy in every nation so many times it's not funny. Democracy is a joke being played on lower income people, and by lower income, I mean people with lower incomes than the Lords of Wall Street.

However, all mass movements that claim to speak for the collective good of the people are

Why Nazism and White Racism Suck

just as phony as democracy. Socialism, communism, fascism, Nazism, and so on are just as full of shit as democracy is. Who are these people that they claim to represent? The Left claims to speak for the working class, but do they?

In America, the most Left-wing places are the West Coast, the East Coast, and the big cities, while the most Right-wing places are rural and small-town America. Why is this? It's because money rules the West Coast, the East Coast, and the big cities, while rural and small-town America is less affluent.

The American working class is and always has been, generally speaking, to the Right, while the affluent classes have always been the breeding grounds of the Left.

Marxism didn't grow from the German working class, but from the German universities where the prosperous drank fine wine and dreamed of changing the world into their personal socialist fantasies. The working class never dreamed up Communism; the affluent university students and professors did. The same is true with the American Left. Outside of affluent university elitists, you are hard-pressed to find many Marxists. I grew up in a working-class oil-lease village. Most of these people were fundamentalist Christians who were just two steps to the right of Attila the Hun.

At the age of twelve, I joined the Young Socialist Alliance, the Communist youth group of the Trotskyite Socialist Worker's Party. The main duty of a YSA member was to pay lots of dues and to also buy (with your own money) lots of copies of the Party's two newspapers, the Young Socialist and the Militant, sell the newspapers to the working class, then send all the profits back to the national headquarters in New York City. At twelve, I would walk up to redneck oilfield workers and try to sell them copies of The Young Socialist and The Militant. It took no time to realize that, even though these two newspapers both claimed to be "The Voice of the Working Class," they were not. Oilfield workers don't dream of the dictatorship of the proletariat. Marxism is something the comfortable university-intelligentsia fantasize about in fraternity houses at Yale and Princeton.

National Socialism is the voice of the Aryan race, but who outside of National Socialism calls themselves The Aryan Race? Are only Nazis members of the Aryan race? The White racist movement claims to speak for the

Why Nazism and White Racism Suck

White race, but then why do most Whites hate the White racist movement? The White racist movement is not the voice of the White race any more than Marxism is the voice of the working class or that democracy is the voice of the people. All collective movements that claim to speak for the masses are full of crap because the masses don't have a single opinion about anything. Shit, most human beings don't have a single opinion about anything outside of what television and public schools tell them to think. You can't be the voice of the people because the people don't have a singular mind.

All mass movements suck because the masses are allowed to join them.

All collective movements desire to control the state in order to control the masses. None of them really wish to liberate the masses because, honestly, how can you liberate them? You can control them. You can tell them how to live their lives, but how can anyone liberate someone else? People have to liberate themselves. You can force morality on people, but this just creates other problems.

The American Volstead Act, which enacted prohibition in the United States, is a great

example. The Christian women's groups
behind the Volstead Act had good intentions.
Alcoholism was wrecking the American family
in the early 1900s. However, as George
Bernard Shaw said, the road to hell is paved
with good intentions. Accordingly, Prohibition
led the nation to hell. It didn't stop
alcoholism. On the contrary, people drank
more during Prohibition because people don't
like to be told what to do. They revolted
against the Volstead Act and drank until the
'20s roared. Morality has to be an individual
choice. You should preach morality, but be
careful when you try to enforce it. Laws often
backfire.

The racist movement is dead in the water
because Hitler took power. Before Hitler,
America and the West were very racial.
However, only about 2% or 3% of the
population were actual die-hard bigoted
racists. By racial, I mean White people were
happy to be White. Non-Whites were happy to
be non-White. You can love your own race
without hating others. You should love your
race without hating others. Generally, this is
called being racial or racialism. Everything
has a dark side, and the dark side of
racialism is racism. Racists hate other
people. Racialists love their own people. Two
very different things. Leftists claim there is

Why Nazism and White Racism Suck

no difference between racialism and racism, but this is bullshit. I would rather meet ten Black men in a dark alley who were racialists that loved the Black race but didn't hate White people, than meet ten Black militant racists in a dark alley who hated me because I am White. People who think there is no difference between racial pride and racial hate are morons.

America before Hitler was full of people proud to be White, but a small vocal minority of those people hated non-Whites. These racists disgraced and helped destroy White pride in America. However, the worst thing to ever happen to the White race was Adolf Hitler. I know you see Hitler as the greatest White man who ever lived, but he was not.

In actual fact, Hitler, like most liberals, didn't believe there was a White race. He believed in the Aryan race. To Hitler, and most of the people in the National Socialist movement, this meant Germanic, and it didn't mean Celtic, Baltic, Slavic, Balkan, Greco-Roman, Hispanic, nor any other White ethnic group. The Third Reich was not pro-White. It persecuted and murdered many White people simply because they weren't ethnic Germans.

Why Nazism and White Racism Suck

In Mein Kampf, Hitler praises the Germanic British and attacked the Celtic Irish, while claiming the Irish and the Negro are the only two races that create their own ghettoes.

In his book, The Myth of the 20th Century, the National Socialist ideologue, Dr. Alfred Rosenberg wrote that "no consideration" for Poles, Czechs, and other "subhuman Slavs" would be taken. Rosenberg's writing, like those of Karl Marx, caused immense human suffering. Whereas Marx was a universalist and his writings caused universal suffering across the globe, Rosenberg was a hyper-racist, and his writings mainly caused the death of White people. Marxists aren't prejudice; they'll murder people of any race. The Nazis were racist; they mainly murdered people of European ancestry. How in the fuck do you see Hitler and Nazism as pro-White? They harmed the White race. What earthly good is an ideology that teaches one White ethnic group to hate all other White ethnic groups?

Hitler and his ilk were not heroes of the White race, but it's furthermost traitors.

This system sucks because it is ruled by tricks and lies. The real power in America has always been in the hands of a few thousand

Why Nazism and White Racism Suck

people. Democracy is too oppressive. Why in hell do you want more government? Socialism is just more government. All governments on the Left, the Right, and the Center mean oligarchies. Communism, fascism, socialism, Nazism, and liberal democracy are all oligarchies, which hide behind a wall of propaganda. They all try to convince the masses that they are "really" in power. Democracy is better at fooling the sheep. However, all governments that claim they are "of the people" are full of shit.

Democracy is a kinder, gentler imperiousness, but it still is a rich man's autarchy that controls the masses. Democracy is a more "caring" tyranny than National Socialism. Why do you want to exchange this creepy, soft-spoken, Mr. Rogers' repression for a brighter, Whiter, and meaner domination? Is there nothing better than having someone else's boot pressed against your throat? Why do you need the state? Why can't you empower yourself and your family? Why does everyone on the Left, the Right, and the Center turn to government to solve their problems? Why does mankind need a FDR, a JFK, a Reagan, a Hitler, a Bush, an Obama, and so forth to save them?

Hitler is the answer for people who can't save

Why Nazism and White Racism Suck

themselves.

Before Hitler, the West was racial, until
some group of racist assholes put Hitler in
power. Hitler had around ten million people
murdered. After World War II, the
communists and capitalists used these
murders for propaganda purposes.
Communists murdered over 100 million
people, but the Communists and the
capitalists saw no propaganda value in these
crimes. Therefore, the masses know nothing
about them. However, the murders the Nazis
committed have propaganda value, so the
masses know all about them. The exposure of
these murders have brought great shame and
disgrace on the racist movement as it
deserves to being shamed and disgraced.

Sadly, the mass murders the Communists
committed have no value for this system, and
Leftists have not had to pay the public
dishonor they so rightly deserve to pay.

Public opinion is created by propaganda.
Money controls propaganda. Exposing the
crimes of the Left doesn't advance the agenda
of money. Therefore, the cattle will never
know the magnitude of the killings the Left
wing committed. This is just how our
democracy works. We can't change

Why Nazism and White Racism Suck

democracy since we are not the moneyed elite. This is just how it goes.

Hitler has brought great shame on your movement and on the entire White race. Why do you worship him like a god? Do you like the fact that this asshole killed White pride, perhaps forever? Are you happy that Hitler murdered millions of innocent White people?

If some Black thug murders a White family, you are enraged, but Hitler murdered millions of White families, and he is your hero. Why is that?

If a Black thug murdered a White family and said he did it for the greater good of the Aryan Race, would he be your hero, too?

The Left loves Hitler because he is a horrible bull-whip they can beat the White race with. Hitler can't be defended against because he was a monster. If democracy was a system of truth, the Left would also be endlessly flogged by the crimes of Lenin, Trotsky, Stalin, Mao, Pol Pot, Che, Castro, and the others. Sorrowfully, democracy isn't a system of truth, but a system of money. The Left will never be publicly shamed for what they have done.

Why Nazism and White Racism Suck

Luckily, the racist movement is held up to a higher standard than the Left. The crimes of Hitler and National Socialism have been exposed. Hitler and Nazism are dead. The racist movement will never again get into power and murder people. I wish I could say the same thing about the Leftists.

Chapter Two

The Appeal of Totalitarian Cults

Totalitarian cults appeal to people who have no hope and who have no voice. People who have hope and a voice don't dream of being cogs in a dictatorship run by someone else. You know your life is pretty fucked up when your sterling aspiration is to join a revolutionary movement and fight to give someone else total power over your life. National Socialism is the strongest segment of the racist movement in America. So, I will focus largely on N.S. (National Socialism).

National Socialism, Marxian Socialism, and even liberal democracy are all totalitarian cults that promise to empower the people, while, in truth, centralize all power in the hands of a few. The biggest difference between National Socialism and Marxian Socialism is the Nazis hate the Jews, while the Communists, traditionally, hate the rich.

In spite of this, nowadays, the Left has transferred their hate from the rich onto the White working class. They hate rednecks, pecker-woods, trailer trash, small-town Christians, Tea Partiers, and everyone else they see as part of the "privileged" White underclass.

I was active in the American Left for nine years. One of the most amazing things about the Left is they hated my people for all being a bunch of green-teethed, uneducated, pig-fucking, poor White trash, bigoted rednecks at the very same time they hated us for being "privileged" because of our White skin. We were all "privileged poor White trash, living in trailer parks" and we were the ones "who controlled the capitalist system." No wonder the Left hates us so.

Totalitarian cults make things clear. They lie a lot, but their real power is they tell an untold truth no one else is willing to speak. They promise to help people that no one else gives a shit about. Communism has always been full of shit. Marxists distort history.

Why Nazism and White Racism Suck

They claim up is down and down is up.
However, they have always addressed real
problems no one else was willing to address.

The same is true with the National Socialists.
Nazism has always been as full of shit as
Communism. However, like the Left, they
attract people by speaking truths no one else
will speak.

For instance, German War Guilt was a load
of crap. Germany didn't start World War One.
It was started equally by German, Turkish,
Italian, French, English, Russian, and
American imperialism. However, after the
war ended and Germany lost, the League of
Nations blamed defeated Germany for
starting the war. They made Germany pay so
much of the war debt that the League of
Nations caused a great German depression
backed up by hyper-inflation.

Hitler and the Nationalsozialistische
Deutsche Arbeiterparte (The National
Socialist German Workers' Party) were the
only ones to strongly oppose "German war
guilt" and the rightfully hated League of
Nations. During the 1920s, "war guilt" helped
create the Nazi Party just as White guilt, the
system' s hate for White working-class
people, and their lack of sympathy for poor

23

Why Nazism and White Racism Suck

Whites, is helping to create a new National Socialist movement today.

Radical movements feed off of one another just as the system in power uses them as chess pieces to control the board.

During World War One, Germany wanted Russia out of the war, so they put the Communist leader Lenin on a train and helped him sneak back into Russia in order to cause the Czar problems. Even the United States got into the act. Wilson saw Russia as an easily removable competitor in the world empire business, and Wall Street saw communism as a weapon they could use in their international money games. So, the U.S. and its master, Wall Street, helped the Communists get into power and stay in power. The U.S. played well, and we have an American empire today.

In 1919, the Communists started a failed revolution in Germany. While the Marxists controlled Berlin, they executed many hundreds of German anti-Communists. This news didn't set well with the average German, who was not fond of the idea of being executed by Leftists.

After Russia fell to the Reds, numerous non-

Why Nazism and White Racism Suck

Communists escaped the Marxist tyranny and ended up in Western Europe. Many settled in Germany in the 1920s, and their stories of Communist atrocities spread like wildfire. The German people were terrified of the Leftists taking over their nation and for damn good reasons. The Reds were mass murderers.

The National Socialists used this reasonable fear of Communism to make Hitler seem like Germany's only hope for sanity. Most Germans who supported Hitler weren't Nazis; they were just people afraid of the Communists committing the same mass murders in Germany as they committed in Russia.

They were also people who wanted to feed their families. The League of Nations caused hunger and great poverty in Germany.

Hitler used this fear of Marxist atrocities to commit his own crimes against humanity.

After World War Two, the Marxists used German guilt over the holocaust to bully their way into German society. In the 1960s, the Leftists learned they could use White guilt over slavery, mistreatment of American Indians, and others to bully their way into

Why Nazism and White Racism Suck

power in America. The Marxists use charges of racism and "White privilege" to get power all over the West.

You, young White racist, are the greatest tool the radical Left has in capturing the West. They are always giving you free publicity because racism empowers the Left. They use you racists just like Hitler used the Communists to take power.

Why do you want to be a racist tool?

Chapter Three

Racist Ideology is Fucking Stupid

Racist ideology is fucking stupid, and I don't mean this from a liberal and anti-White perspective. From a strictly pro-White standpoint, what passes as racist thought is insane.

Racist Ethnic Theory

Let's look at ethnic theories. Racist ethnic theory is full-blown race treason. Starting out with Joseph Arthur Comte de Gobineau's *An Essay on the Inequality of the Human Races*, which defames the Slavic peoples, up to Professor Hans Friedrich Karl Günther's *The Racial Elements of European History*, which defames all White people except tall slender blonds, all ethnic theories are racial treason.

27

Why Nazism and White Racism Suck

Hans F. K. Günther and Rosenberg were the two main racial theoreticians of the Third Reich.

Hans F. K. Günther goes as far as dividing White Germans into six different races. Here is what he wrote about the Nordic:

"The skull of the Nordic man likewise grows narrow, long. The face is small. The breadth in proportion to length is as 3 to 4. The shape of the face is striking, not unaccentedly round. The nose is high set. In proportion to the rest of the face it is likewise small. If it is indented then this occurs in the upper third in contrast to the Dinaric and north Asiatic races. The skin is light, rosy-white, and delicate. In contrast to the skin of many other races it is distinguished by a lack of pigmentation. The hair is smooth, wavy, thin, and fine. Its colour varies from light to golden blond. As to eyes we distinguish the colouring primarily according to the colours of the iris. The Nordic race has light coloured eyes, blue, blue-grey to grey. In what follows we shall see still further how the bodily characteristics of the Nordic race are distinguishable from those of other races. Such distinctions also apply in the case of the internal organs. There are, for example, differences in the structure and size of the brain and the bodily glands. Mental and spiritual differences are naturally related thereto. In dealing with traits of mind and soul even more

28

than in dealing with bodily characteristics we must concentrate upon entire groups of people belonging to a particular race rather than upon individual representatives of this race. Now what distinguishes the Nordic race from all others? It is uncommonly gifted mentally. It is outstanding for truthfulness and energy. Nordic men for the most part possess, even in regard to themselves, a great power of judgement. They incline to be taciturn and cautious. They feel instantly that too loud talking is undignified. They are persistent and stick to a purpose when once they have set themselves to it. Their energy is displayed not only in warfare but also in technology and in scientific research. They are predisposed to leadership by nature."

In other words, if you "ain't" Nordic, you "ain't" shit!

Sloppy seconds goes to the Phalic race. Here's what Hans F. K. Günther said about this supposed race:

"The Phalic race on the average surpasses the Nordic in physical size. It averages in height over 1.75 metres. In contrast to the Nordic it is not a tall and slender race, but rather tall and broad. It acts, therefore, much more forcibly. The skull, however, in contrast to the Nordic skull, is broad faced, although just as long up to the middle of the head. The nose is broader than that of the Nordic race, but proportionately smaller, for example, than that of the East Baltic race. The skin is just like that of the Nordic race, a clear, rosy-white. The hair is likewise blond, perhaps somewhat more reddish. It is, in fact, somewhat stiffer, wavy or even curly. The eyes are light in colour, similar to those of the Nordic race, but more often grey than blue. We see, therefore, that the Nordic and Phalic races are rather alike in all these characteristics. The only difference is that the Phalic race acts more forcibly, dynamically, as Gunther once said. Similarly, differences in the soul qualities of the two races are not very great. The Phalic man is less emotional than the Nordic man. He is said to be better suited for being the driving force under the leadership of Nordic men than for leadership himself. Great patience characterises his pursuit of an aim. Never could he be as fool-hardy, perhaps, as Nordic man. He is governed by a strong feeling of loyalty toward other men. He is more good natured and more cordial than the Nordic man."

In third place is the Western or Western Alpine race, here is what the Nutty Professor Günther says about them:

"The skull is long and small faced. It is similar, therefore, to the skull of the Nordic race. It is not, however, angular. The chin is not so pronounced. The head is smaller in comparison to the size of the body than is that of the Nordic race. The nose is not proportionately so high. The skin is not light, but tinted. It is uniformly brown. The hair is

Why Nazism and White Racism Suck

like that of the Nordic, fine and smooth, and also curly. It is oily. The colour varies from dark brown to black. The eyes likewise vary from brown to dark brown. Compared to the Nordic race there are great differences in soul qualities. The men of the Western race are much more ready to talk, lively, even loquacious. In comparison to the Nordic and Phalic men they have much less patience or steadiness. They act more by feeling than by reason. The difficult and burdensome are repugnant to the man of the Western race. He is excitable, even passionate. The Western race with all its mental agility lacks creative power. This race has produced only a few outstanding men."

Hey, Hans F. K. Günther doesn't sound like he was out of his fucking mind, does he?

In fourth place among the White people of Germany are the Dinaric race. Here is what Günther wrote:

"This race has few similarities to the Nordic so far as bodily structure is concerned. In Germany we find these people in the south and south-west as well as in central Germany. In Europe outside of the Reich we encounter them in England, in the eastern Alpine lands (they are named after the Dinaric Alps) and in the Balkans as far as the Ukraine. The size of body approximates that of the Nordic race. The Dinaric man is, on the average, 1.74 metres tall. He is tall and slender. The skull is both small faced and short headed.

31

Why Nazism and White Racism Suck

The back of the head scarcely rises above the neck. The nose is very high and large. It is often very sharply indented. The skin is brownish. The texture of the hair is fine, curly. In contrast to other races bodily hair is also well developed. Its colouring is brownish-black to black. The eyes are dark-brown to very dark. So far as mind and soul are concerned the Dinaric man has some outstanding attributes. Like the Nordic he is very proud and unceasingly brave. He is a good warrior. His love for homeland is great. He is equipped with more creative ability than the neighbouring Eastern man. In contrast to the Nordic the Dinaric is much more subject to his moods. He is noisier by nature, more loquacious. Great thought processes and investigations are not in him. He does have, however, a great gift for music."

In fifth place is the Eastern or Eastern Alpine race. Let's see what National Socialism says about them:

"So far as physical size is concerned the Eastern man is also not as large as the Nordic man. The man has as average height of 1.63 metres. Although he is, therefore, almost as tall as the members of the Western race, yet in physical makeup he is, as to them and as to the Nordic race, the exact opposite. He is thick-set, compact, clumsy. His shape is broad based. He reaches sexual maturity early, but also grows old very early. The breadth of shoulders and smallness of hips, characteristic of the Nordic man, are, in his case, not pronounced. the legs are, in proportion to the length of the body, rather short. In contrast to the Nordic and Western man, as well as the East Baltic man, he is rather heavy. His skull is short, wide-faced, round. It has scarcely any very pronounced lines. The skull width and length relate as 9 to 10. The ratio is quite unlike that in the case of the skull of the Nordic man (3 to 4). The nose is sunk low, less sharply drawn. The skin is yellow-brown to yellowish. It is not so delicate as that of the Nordic race. The hair is thicker and tighter. It is stiff. In colour it varies from dark brown to black. The eyes are brown. In spiritual attitude great differences exist between the Eastern and the Nordic men. The former are, to be sure, courageous, but not rash and bold. They are unwarlike. They incline to craftiness. They lack the spirit of rulers. For this reason they are compliant and submissive subjects. The Eastern race is always the led, never the leader. Its capacity for holding together large communities seldom stands out."

And at the bottom of the German people, the Nazis put the East Baltic Race:

"The East Baltic man is, on the average, 1.64 metres tall. The growth is similar to that of the Eastern race. The East Baltic man is merely more energetic. He is, to be sure, short and large boned. He is broad based. The man has great breadth of shoulders. In fullness of body he is quite like the Eastern man. Although he seems to

33

mature rather late; yet, in spite of that, he begins to age early. The skull is like that of the Easterner, short, wide-faced. It is, however, more angular and bonier. Remarkable is the size of the face in relation to the size of the brain. The nose is sunk low, rather broad. The skin is light, grey-yellow. The hair is thick and coarse, stiff. Its colour is ash-blond, but can have a grey undertone. In youth the colour of the hair can be very like that of the Nordic race. The eyes are grey, blue-grey to water-blue. Little as yet is known about the soul qualities of East Baltic men. They are no leaders, by nature, but need leadership. They, in contrast to the Nordic man, are without a real power of decision in conflicts of conscience. And so they are always cautious, never resolute. Their power of imagination is roving, unsteady. Creatively, they are best in the field of music."

This is what Hitler and the National Socialist movement thought of the German people. If you weren't tall and blond, you were inferior and had to be ruled by the jack boots of the Nordic race. Do you genuinely believe that White Germans are divided into six separate races? And remember, this is just what the Nazi kooks thought about Germany; they thought less of most other White nations. If you are not tall, slender, and blond, why would you be into this bullshit? Do you really think you are not as good as the mythical Nordic race? What purpose does it serve the

Why Nazism and White Racism Suck

White race to divide our people up into a
bunch of races that only crackpots believe
exist? There's a White race. There is no such
thing as a Phalic race, a Western race, or an
Eastern race. There is only a White race.

Following Professor Hans F. K. Günther's
racist theories, my father had black hair and
was a member of the Dinaric race. My mother
had reddish hair, and according to Hitler's
book, Mein Kampf, the redheaded Celts,
along with the Negroes, were among the only
two races that create their own ghettoes. My
parents, according to Nazi ideology, were
from two separate races: the Dinaric race and
the Celtic race. My parents had five kids. The
three olders boys were members of the
Western Alpine race. My sister was a member
of the Eastern Alpine race, and my little
brother was a member of the Nordic race. So,
according to National Socialism, my parents
were from two different races and by "race
mixing" they created five children who were
members of three separate races other than
their own. How the fuck did that happen? If a
Black man marries a Chinese woman, they
don't create three Mexicans, an American
Indian, and a blond Icelander. Do they? Hell,
no! This would be impossible. Nazi racist
theory is nuts.

Why Nazism and White Racism Suck

Nazism is race treason.

All this stupid racist theory did was cause the "Nordic" S.S. to murder "inferior" Whites in Eastern Europe and elsewhere.

Do you really believe blonds are better than Whites with red, brown, or black hair?

Speaking as a racially inferior Western Alpine, I would like to say, fuck your racist theories!

The Jewish Question

Ah, the Jewish question. In Joseph Arthur Comte de Gobineau's *An Essay on the Inequality of the Human Races*, he classified the Jews as members of the Aryan race. Traditionally, in Europe, Jews weren't hated for their race. The Catholic Church hated the Jews because they rejected Christ. Early racists saw anti-Semitism as just a Christian thing, until Karl Marx wrote a book called *On the Jewish Question*. Here is what the German Karl Marx's wrote about his fellow Jews.

"Let us consider the actual, worldly Jew – not the *Sabbath Jew*, as Bauer does, but the *everyday*

Why Nazism and White Racism Suck

Jew.

Let us not look for the secret of the Jew in his religion, but let us look for the secret of his religion in the real Jew.

What is the secular basis of Judaism? *Practical need, self-interest.* What is the worldly religion of the Jew? *Huckstering.* What is his worldly God? *Money.*

Very well then! Emancipation from *huckstering* and *money,* consequently from practical, real Judaism, would be the self-emancipation of our time.

An organization of society which would abolish the preconditions for huckstering, and therefore the possibility of huckstering, would make the Jew impossible. His religious consciousness would be dissipated like a thin haze in the real, vital air of society. On the other hand, if the Jew recognizes that this *practical* nature of his is futile and works to abolish it, he extricates himself from his previous development and works for *human emancipation* as such and turns against the supreme practical expression of human self-estrangement.

We recognize in Judaism, therefore, a general *anti-social* element of the *present time,* an element which through historical development – to which in this harmful respect the Jews have zealously contributed – has been brought to its present

37

high level, at which it must necessarily begin to disintegrate.

In the final analysis, the *emancipation of the Jews* is the emancipation of mankind from *Judaism*.

The Jew has already emancipated himself in a Jewish way.

'The Jew, who in Vienna, for example, is only tolerated, determines the fate of the whole Empire by his financial power. The Jew, who may have no rights in the smallest German state, decides the fate of Europe. While corporations and guilds refuse to admit Jews, or have not yet adopted a favorable attitude towards them, the audacity of industry mocks at the obstinacy of the material institutions.' (Bruno Bauer, *The Jewish Question*, p. 114)

This is no isolated fact. The Jew has emancipated himself in a Jewish manner, not only because he has acquired financial power, but also because, through him and also apart from him, *money* has become a world power and the practical Jewish spirit has become the practical spirit of the Christian nations. The Jews have emancipated themselves insofar as the Christians have become Jews."

While Joseph Arthur Comte de Gobineau saw anti-Semitism as just a Christian thing, and he placed Jews among the Aryan race, Karl Marx saw Judaism as a bogus religion used

38

as a front to hide the "Jewish race's" true religion: money.

I disagree with many things Arthur de Gobineau wrote, but he was, partly, right about the Jews. Many Jews are members of the Aryan race. However, some Jews are part of the Black race, the Chinese race, etc. Judaism is a religion, not a race. Karl Marx was a twisted man, whose writings led directly to the murder of over 100 million innocent people.

Karl Marx was the voice of socialism in Germany. Marx was an atheist. He didn't hate the Jews for killing Christ. He hated them for being a race of hucksters. Karl Marx helped spread racial anti-Semitism through German Socialism. From Marx's time up to the Third Reich, German Nationalism and German Socialism cross pollinated, until Hitler fused the two together and created National Socialism. Karl Marx helped make racial anti-Semitism part of German Socialism.

Whereas de Gobineau saw anti-Semitism as just Christian nonsense, Houston Stewart Chamberlain picked up Karl Marx's racial anti-Semitic ball and ran with it. In Chamberlain's book, *The Foundations of the*

Why Nazism and White Racism Suck

Nineteenth Century, he placed the Jew as a
race in direct conflict with the Aryan. Karl
Marx saw the Jews as a race of evil money
worshippers. Chamberlain agreed with Marx.
The materialistic Jews were the antithesis of
the noble Aryans.

Houston Stewart Chamberlain's book led to
Dr. Alfred Rosenberg writing the Nazi Bible,
The Myth of the 20th Century, and
Rosenberg's book led to the holocaust.

Hitler Worship

Hitler Worship is one step below devil
worship. Why do you need to worship Hitler?
It is for the same reason people on the Left
need to worship Chairman Mao, Che, Stalin,
and other evil people. Evil is cool. Evil
worship is a rebellion against society. In the
1920s, kids drank bootlegged gin to embrace
evil and to shock society and their parents. In
the 1950s, people idolized Elvis in order to be
evil and to shock society and their parents. In
the 1960s, kids grew their hair long and
became hippies to shock society. In the
1970s, Satanism and punk rock became the
great rebellion. However, by the 1980s,
society had seen it all. There were no more
social taboos kids could break to shock

society. It had all been done before. Or had it? Neo-Nazism and racism were the last breakable taboos in Politically Correct liberal society. Long hair, Mohawks, strange music, and so on no longer shocked society. They learned to tolerate everything but racism. Boom! Racism and Nazism became the last great act of rebellion against a society that tolerated everything. To love Hitler was to shock the world.

Nazism is the ultimate rebellion against liberal society. Nothing yanks the chains of polite society more than Hitler.

Hitler is the perfect evil to base a youth rebellion on. Nothing gets a reaction like a swastika.

With Hitler, you can get the government, the public schools, the news media, and your parents to go ape-shit. Everyone hates Hitler. How cool is that?

However, for kids who want a more P.C. form of youth rebellion, a good Chairman Mao or Che t-shirt will do the trick. This way, you can be evil and embrace a mass murderer, but P.C. society doesn't give a fuck about how many innocent people the Marxists murdered, so with Mao or Che as your evil

41

daddy, you won't suffer any of the negative backlash as you would with Hitler. Some mass murderers are just more tolerated by liberal society than others.

Christian Identity

Christian Identity is a racist sect that teaches: 1. The Aryans are the noblest of races., 2. Jews are the devil., 3. The Jews are not Aryans., 4. The only good Jew is a dead Jew., 5. The Jews are not really Jews., and 6. The Aryans are the true Jews. (See: 4. The only good Jew is a dead Jew.).

If Christian Identity believes the only good Jew is a dead Jew, and that the Aryan race is the true Jewish race, do Christian Identity people throw themselves into the ovens?

Christian Identity claims to be pro-White, but I have been to the Aryan Nations compound and other Christian Identity meeting places. I never heard anything pro-White and, actually, I can't recall anything very Christian either. Christian Identity is focused not on loving the White race, nor is it focused on loving Jesus Christ, but on hating Blacks, Jews, Mexicans, and others. It's not a love White folks groups, but a hate non-Whites cult.

Christian Identity doesn't spread love for White people or for Jesus, but just spews out hate and violence. How does this help the White race better itself? It doesn't. Hate just misleads young Whites like yourself to do vile and stupid things that cause harm to yourselves, to others, to society, and to our White race. Hate doesn't work.

Anti-Hate Incorporated exaggerated the importance of Christian Identity, and the Anti-Hate groups used their fund-raisers to promote Christian Identity as some mass movement that the Anti-Hate industry needed money to fight: lots and lots of money. In reality, Christian Identity was nothing until it was built up by Anti-Hate, Inc. The Anti-Haters needed Christian Identity and the racist movement to profit. Therefore, they made the racist movement famous and newsworthy.

Naval Commander George Lincoln Rockwell and The American Nazi Party

In the 1950s, the American Nazi Party (ANP) was founded by U.S. Naval Commander

Why Nazism and White Racism Suck

George Lincoln Rockwell, who, shortly before starting the American Nazi Party, worked in Naval Intelligence and Counter Intelligence. The American Nazi Party Headquarters were in Arlington, Virginia, just a short distance from the FBI, CIA, and other U.S. Intelligence Agencies.

In the 1950s, the FBI and other government organizations often used its agents to create fake "resistance" groups on both the Left and the Right in order to watch, control, and keep down radical movements. If a movement appeared to be growing, undercover agents in the leadership position would do something that would sabotage the movements' chances of success.

George Lincoln Rockwell advocated a strategy of shock propaganda. Rockwell called his group the American Nazi Party to shock and outrage people.

American Nazi Party members were mostly dummkopfs from prisons, mental institutions, and their parents' basements. Rockwell dressed his troops up in Nazi uniforms and marched them up and down the streets like circus clowns to shock and enrage the average White American by chanting harebrained things like "Six million more! Six million more! Six million more!"

It seemed as if someone had paid Rockwell to disgrace the White Cause.

Rockwell dressed in a Nazi Commander uniform. His Revenge of the Nerds rejects dressed as S.S. Storm Troopers. They held up signs for the TV news cameras and chanted crazy things like *"Roses are red, violets are blue, when we come to power, it's to the ovens with you!"*

White Americans watching TV at home weren't impressed by Rockwell and his gay jamboree of Storm Troopers.

Rockwell dressed in Nazi uniforms that many Americans had fought against in World War II, or they had friends and loved ones who died fighting against the Nazis. Rockwell slapped the American people in the face with his Nazism. The American people weren't happy with Rockwell.

They were entirely pissed off and enraged when Rockwell and his Storm Troopers held signs up and chanted "... when we come to power, it's to the ovens with you!"

Rockwell and his American Nazi Party

pushed away White America. Rockwell prevented normal White people from joining even the mildest pro-White cause because Rockwell helped disgrace the White cause in America.

Perhaps, this is what the government was paying Rockwell to do.

What do the French call these people? Agent provocateurs! People who go into a movement to mislead and destroy it from within.

Anti-Hate Incorporated exaggerated the importance of Commander George Lincoln Rockwell and the American Nazi Party, and they used their fund-raisers to promote Rockwell as some terrifying boogeyman that Anti-Hate profiteers needed money to fight. In reality, George Lincoln Rockwell and the American Nazi Party were nothing until he and his fellow kooks were built up by Anti-Hate, Inc.

Dr. David Duke and the Ku Klux Klan

After George Lincoln Rockwell was shot and killed, the American Nazi Party was taken over by a man who turned it into a private cult, which fell from the limelight. The next big star on the American racist movement was David Duke and his Knights of the Ku Klux Klan.

David Duke was a student of Rockwell. Duke picked up where Rockwell left off, and Dr. Duke became the new master of shock propaganda.

In the 1970s and early '80s, Duke would say that just by being in the Klu Klux Klan all you have to do is show up in a Klan robe to get free publicity from the liberal news media. There was an entire industry raking in billions of dollars fighting hate. They loved fighting hate. It was their gravy train. The anti-hate industry formed "non-profit" tax exemption charitable organizations that collected tax deductible donations from affluent liberals. The heads of these "altruistic" organizations could pay their leaders (often themselves) six figure salaries and also buy them properties, jets, limousines, yachts, clothing, and much more all in the name of the non-profit organization. Oh, yes, they also fought hate. This meant they sent out press releases, asked for more donations, wrote reports, collected more funds, collected speaking fees, went on TV and radio and promoted their organization,

47

asked for more donations, created hysteria about tiny hate groups, asked for more donations, and occasionally fought a few court cases against some ignorant saps who couldn't afford attorneys.

These anti-hate groups needed hate groups to bring in the cash, and the hate groups needed the anti-hate industry for free publicity and to help convince the masses that these Nazi and Klan groups were more than just some guy with a post office box.

The hate groups and Anti-Hate, Incorporated made beautiful music together, and it was a marriage made in heaven. A Win-Win for both haters and anti-haters.

The Ku Klux Klan was famous for lynching Black people. It had disgraced itself, and no self-respecting White person would ever join it. David Duke was dead in the water the minute he put on a Klan robe, but he didn't care. The hate movement is not about helping the White race. It is about making any pro-White cause look stupid and evil, and of course, it's also about helping the Left wing raise money.

Anti-Hate Incorporated exaggerated the importance of Dr. David Duke and his various organizations, and they used their fund raisers to promote Duke as some formidable boogeyman the anti-hate industry needed money to fight. In reality, Dr. David Duke was nothing until he was built up by Anti-Hate, Inc.

Dr. William Luther Pierce and the National Alliance

Dr. William Pierce got his PhD in nuclear physics. It is common for crackpots to have PhDs. It's unnerving when they get one in nuclear physics. Great evil comes from the universities. Communism grew out of the German universities, and most universities in the West are controlled by Marxists.

The Khmer Rouge murdered between 20% to 37% of the Cambodian population. The blood-thirsty leaders of the Khmer Rouge (Pol Pot, Ieng Sary, Khieu Samphan, Hou Yuon, Son Sen, Khieu Ponnary, and Khieu Thirith), learned the teachings of Marx, Lenin, and Mao while they were students at the University of Paris. While in Paris living off scholarships funded by European liberals, these soon to be mass murderers joined the French Communist Party and fit right in with the French intelligentsia.

Why Nazism and White Racism Suck

Like the French intellectuals who went on to
create the Khmer Rouge, Dr. William Pierce
went to a university. Dr. Pierce founded the
National Alliance, which was the White
American doppelganger of the Khmer Rouge.
Luckily, for us, the intellectuals at the
National Alliance never took power. I wish the
Cambodian people would have had the same
luck with the Khmer Rouge.

 Dr. William Pierce created the violent cult,
the National Alliance, and built it's
compound in West Virginia because he knew
the local hillbillies would be impressed with
his PhD, which is the same reason the
Southern Poverty Law Center has its
headquarters in Montgomery, Alabama. The
big frog in a small pond effect.

Dr. Pierce wrote a revolutionary novel called
The Turner Diaries, which was structured on
Jack London's *The Iron Heel*. However,
Pierce's novel is a lot more violent than
London's. *The Turner Diaries* advocates
violent revolution in the United States:
bombings of government buildings, terrorist
attacks on nuclear power plants, the "Day of
the Rope" where Jews, race traitors, and non-
Whites are executed, and finally, victory for
the White race comes with nuclear terrorism

that kicks off a nuclear war between the U.S. and Russia. In the real world, this scenario of terrorists kicking off a nuclear holocaust that destroys both the United States and, at the time, the Soviet government would just leave the door open for a Red Chinese invasion of the entire West and really screw the White race.

The Turner Diaries has given birth to a number of terrorists, terrorist groups, and simple murders committed by racists captivated by Dr. Pierce's PhD.

The Turner Diaries states that this race war will cost the lives of over 60 million people. This is manslaughter on the scale of Marxism.

Communist China murdered between 60 million to 80 million of it's own people. The Cambodian version of the National Alliance, the Khmer Rouge, murdered about a third of its own people. Why would you want to cause such death? What good would it do the White race if you caused the death of so many people? Do you really need mass murder to change the world?

Revolutionaries with PhDs so often cause crimes against humanity. The American

Why Nazism and White Racism Suck

Revolution was not started in the universities, but by businessmen, investors, plantation owners, and land speculators. It committed many crimes against people, but nothing like the revolutions that were started by intellectuals. The French Revolution was started by middle class intellectuals. It was much more savage than the American Revolution. Marxism is the product of universities. The Russian Revolution, the Chinese Revolution, the Cuban Revolution, the Cambodian Revolution, and other socialist revolutions were the most murderous in history.

The National Socialist Revolution always had intellectuals and German academia circling around the leadership. Intellectuals justify everything the movement did. Be careful of joining any movement that has too many people with university degrees. It can come to no good.

Anti-Hate Incorporated exaggerated the importance of Dr. William Luther Pierce and the National Alliance. The marketers used their fund-raisers to hype Pierce as some perilous bugaboo the "civil rights" leaders needed money to fight.

In reality, Dr. William Luther Pierce and the

National Alliance were nothing and never would have been anything, until they were built up by Anti-Hate, Inc.

Robert Jay Mathews and The Order

Robert Jay Mathews was a Mormon. He joined a Mormon survivalist group called the Sons of Liberty. Someone slipped him a copy of *The Turner Diaries*, and Robert Mathews became spellbound by Dr. Pierce's PhD.

Bob Mathews joined the National Alliance.

Mathews soon became disenchanted with the good Doctor. Like most revolutionary intellectuals, Dr. Pierce was more into getting other less scholarly people to do the actual violence. Dr. Pierce was more into thinking of ways to get others to commit crimes. It was around this time Dr. Pierce earned the nickname Dr. Puss or Dr. Pussy because many thought the good Doctor was a coward.

Robert Mathews left the National Alliance, took *The Turner Diaries*, and founded the terrorist group, The Order.

The idea was that they would wake up the White race through direct action and by propaganda of the deed. The Order robbed banks. It robbed an armored truck, and it killed a few people. The majority of White people still have never heard of The Order, while most of the people who know about it are turned off by its senseless violence. The Order did no good. It only took other people's money, got a few people killed, got most of its members long prison sentences, and turned off the few White people who ever heard about it.

Violence is not the correct path.

Ben Klassen and The Church of the Creator

Ben Klassen became rich after he invented the electric can opener. Klassen was born in the Ukraine, into the tyranny of "Uncle Joe" Stalin's socialist Russia. Stalin hated the Ukrainian people. "Uncle Joe" took most the grain grown in the Ukraine and had it shipped and stored in Eastern Russia where it was not needed.

Taking the grain harvest away from the Ukrainian people had the effect that Stalin desired. Between seven and twelve million Ukrainians died of hunger.

Why Nazism and White Racism Suck

Klassen was a little boy in the Ukraine during Stalin's famine. I guess it makes sense for someone who suffered through Stalin's great famine to invent an electric can opener, so folks can get to food faster. Food played a major role in much of Klassen's thoughts. He wrote a lot about salt, sugar, meat, and vegetables. When I first read Klassen, I didn't understand why he spent so much time writing about food, but once I learned about his childhood, I understood.

The memories of Stalin's great famine altered his world view. Ben Klassen was militantly, and rightly so, anti-Communist.

Klassen's family moved to The United States. As a young adult, Klassen became active in anti-Communist movements. Klassen was elected a Florida state legislator as a strong anti-Communist. Many anti-Communists noticed the high percentage of Jews active in Communism. Ben Klassen also noticed this and became very anti-Jewish. Klassen believed the Jews were behind Stalin's starving to death of millions of Ukrainians.

It's true that many Jews are Marxists. However, it is also true that most Jews aren't Marxists, as well as most Marxists aren't Jews. Some people have a problem understanding this. Many does not mean "all" nor does it even mean "the majority." Many simply means "many."

Klassen became captivated by the Jewish Question. He soon saw Jews behind not only Communism, but Christianity as well as other movements.

Klassen established the Church of the Creator, which was an extremely anti-Jewish, anti-Christian, anti-religion, atheistic "Church." The COTC's main goal was to combat the belief of "spooks in the sky" and the Jews. Klassen coined the phrase Racial Holy War (RaHoWa).

The problem with Ben Klassen's Church of the Creator is it is founded on hate. Marxism has murdered over 100 million people because it hates successful people, White people, and everyone who is not Politically Correct. National Socialism murdered over ten million people because it hates the Jews, all White people who are not the Nazi Ideal of the Aryan, in addition to hating others. Movements based on hate will murder. You are wrong to idolize people who preach hate. It will get you nowhere and just consume your life along with others. We should build a movement on love for our own people and not

Why Nazism and White Racism Suck

worry about others.

Anti-Hate Incorporated exaggerated the importance of Ben Klassen and his Church of the Creator. The money whores used their fund raisers to promote Klassen as some treacherous boogeyman they needed money to fight. In reality, Ben Klassen and the Church of the Creator were nothing until they were built up by Anti-Hate, Inc.

Anti-Hate Incorporated is more successful in spreading the messages of hate than the hate groups themselves.

The anti-haters' financial success depends on keeping hate alive.

They profit from fighting hate. If hate disappeared, they would be out of business, which is why these groups act as an advertising agency for hate.

If you don't believe me, just go to one of their websites. They are nothing but endless advertisements for hate groups. Racism sells, and Anti-Hate Incorporated is a master merchant.

Tom Metzger and
the White Aryan Resistance

Thomas Metzger joined the John Birch
Society, then the Ku Kluz Klan, then formed
the White American Political Association,
finally the White Aryan Resistance. Metzger
proudly calls the White Aryan Resistance,

"The most racist organization on earth."
Metzger learned shock propaganda
techniques from Commander Rockwell, Dr.
Pierce, and Dr. Duke. He learned how to use
shock propaganda to coax Anti-Hate,
Incorporated to cause the news media to give
him and his insignificant little group millions
of dollars worth of free publicity. The 1980s
were good to Metzger. The anti-hate industry
made Tom Metzger into a superstar. He was
in countless newspapers, magazines, radio
shows, and on every major TV talk show of
the day. He became an American Icon. None
of this would have ever happened if not for
Anti-Hate, Inc. They wrote reports and sent
out fund-raisers that made Tom Metzger an
international celebrity. How would Metzger
have done any of this without the help of
anti-hate profiteers?

The New Left of the 1960s had Abbie

Why Nazism and White Racism Suck

Hoffman, Jerry Rubin, and other radicals use shock propaganda like Rockwell did in the 1950s. They said stupid things like "Kill your parents.," "Don't trust anyone over 30.," and one of the leaders of the New Left threatened to dump truckloads of LSD into the Los Angeles water system in order to poison the city.

The New Left pulled a Metzger and got tons of free publicity by saying something fucking stupid. I don't know how many new recruits they got from threatening to poison the drinking water of L.A., but it did get them on the 6 o'clock news. How very Metzgeresque.

Metzger believed using the "Jews" was easy. He has said it is like playing a piano. When you hit a certain key, the "Jews" start screaming. Their screams let you know you are doing something right.

The problem with Metzger's thinking is he is focused on getting a reaction from the anti-hate industry, and he doesn't care about appealing to the average White person. They are screaming because Metzger and his ilk have done something so fucking stupid that the anti-hate industry realizes they can make a fortune off of anti-hate fundraisers.

Why Nazism and White Racism Suck

The anti-hate industry is not screaming in
anguish, but in delight because Metzger or
some other idiot just made them tons of
money. When Metzger, or whoever, says or
does something amazingly stupid, he doesn't
just cause a tidal wave of anti-hate
fundraisers; These bonehead racists also
cause the average White person to be driven
away. Why do you want White people to be
driven away from your movement? It makes
one wonder whose side you are really on and
whose side "the movement" is really on.

Anti-Hate Incorporated exaggerated the
importance of Tom Metzger and the White
Aryan Resistance, and they used their
fundraisers to promote Metzger as some great
boogeyman the Left needed money to fight. In
reality, Tom Metzger and the White Aryan
Resistance were nothing until they were built
up by Anti-Hate, Inc. Tom Metzger and all
these dopey racist leaders are the cash-cow
that keeps the anti-hate profiteers in
business. They need to build up these clowns
in order to stay in business.

Skinheads

Skinheads evolved out of the punk-rock
movement of the 1960s, '70s, and '80s. The

Why Nazism and White Racism Suck

Left often claims that skinheads came from Jamaica and the Ska music scene because many Blacks in Ska shaved their heads. However, I have known many skinheads, and not a single one came from Ska. The Left is fond of saying many things that are untrue.

There were very few racist skinheads in North America in the mid-1980s, perhaps a few dozen at the most, until the anti-hate industry started sounding-the-alarm. Tom Metzger saw the Left's overreaction to racist skinheads as a great opportunity to get tons of free publicity and tons of free publicity Metzger got.

Tom Metzger talked to newspapers, magazines, went on radio and TV. He boasted about the non-existence "skinhead phenomena." Metzger was everywhere yelling and arguing with representatives of Anti-Hate Incorporated.

The anti-hate marketers gave Metzger and his imaginary army of skinhead supporters so much free publicity that they sparked public interest in the skinhead movement. This anti-hate reaction helped create the skinhead movement and made Tom Metzger a household name.

Why Nazism and White Racism Suck

However, what good did the skinhead movement do the White race? Metzger isn't the voice of the White race. He is just a self-promoting gadfly that drives most White people away from pro-White causes. The anti-hate industry made billions fighting hate. Many people, both White and non-White, died because of skinheads. Most skinheads are so god-damned Nazi that they can't even relate to their own families and friends.

The skinhead movement harms the White race. It makes charlatans in the racist movement famous. It makes people who hate the White race rich by getting them a boogeyman to fight. Skinheads do no good for the survival and advancement of the White race. Why would you be involved in such a movement?

Holocaust Revisionism

The holocaust happened. The National Socialists murdered around ten million people. They murdered about as many non-Jews as they murdered Jews. One mass murder ten times worse than the holocaust is the...is the...is the? Holy shit! The Marxian Socialists murdered over one hundred people, and our faithful friends in liberal academia don't even see these crimes as worthy of a name. Why is this? Why does the holocaust have a name while the murder of over one hundred million people by the Leftist isn't important enough to earn a name? Why are there numerous holocaust museums and not a single museum devoted to all the crimes of Marxism? This liberal society really lets the Left get away with murder. Why?

It's not fair that National Socialists are endlessly publicly condemned for murdering while the Marxian Socialists, who murdered ten times as many people, are never condemn publicly. Hell, most of academia are historical revisionists who deny the Marxists ever killed anyone, or they play the number of killings down to next to nothing. The only reason they do this is because they are Left wing. The Left is very concerned about the crimes committed by the so-called Right wing because they see the Rightists as their enemies. However, the Left does not give a fuck in hell about the crimes committed by the Left because academia sees Leftists as their friends and comrades. Indeed, academia does everything it can to cover up the crimes of the Left, while at the same time, academia harps to death the crimes of the Right, which is why the holocaust is a household word, and it is why almost no one has ever heard of the...of the...of the (nameless) over one hundred million people the Left murdered.

Recently, the Jewish actress, Natalie Portman, was asked by a reporter if she was interested in doing a holocaust movie. Miss Portman responded that the holocaust was not a movie genre she was interested in. You will never hear a Hollywood movie star saying they are not interested in the...in the...in the (over one hundred million people murdered by Marxian Socialists) genre because a crime that isn't even important enough to be given a name sure the fuck isn't important enough to have it's own Hollywood movie genre.

The Left has done everything it could to rewrite history. They flock to the universities because they realize academia controls the masses.

The universities shape the minds of intellectuals. The universities control the minds of doctors, public school teachers, law makers, radio personalities, TV spokespersons, TV journalists, newspaper reporters, magazine editors, movie directors, and every public leader who leads the sheep. Even so-called members of "the Right wing opposition" go to universities and are taught

Why Nazism and White Racism Suck

how to think and what to think by the Left.

The P.C. Right bases its worldview on a scholastic world that is Left wing. Conservatives learned all they know by reading textbooks and history books written by Left-wingers. Conservatives are just a less radical form of the Left. This is where the Neo-Conservatives (Neo-Cons) come from. They base their conservativism on liberal principles. Neo-Conservatives are Economic Capitalists and Social Marxists. As Noam Chomsky said, he knew most the Neo-Con leaders when they were young Trotskyites. The Neo-Cons still are Trotskyites, but they now have replaced international socialism and world democracy with international capitalism and world democracy. The only thing different between a Trotskyite and a Neo-Conservative is economies. This is one reason the Neo-Cons never talk about the crimes of Marxism. With most social issues, they are in basic agreement with the Left, and they still get teary-eyed over their former idols, the Marxist revolutionaries.

The intelligentsia is guilty of negationism. The word "negationism" means to use your scholarly gifts to make crimes against mankind disappear from the history books. All of P.C. academia does this in order to

protect their friends and comrades in the
Left.

Academia covers up the crimes of Marxism
by playing ignorant, underestimating
numbers, disavowing history, rewriting
events, and lying about facts. The great
danger of the academic world is not just that
they cover up past crimes of the Left. The real
threat of academia is by covering up the past
crimes of their friends and comrades that
they are giving them the freedom to commit
more mass murders in the future.

Academia is the ghost of mass murders yet to
come.

After World War II, the National Socialists
saw how their fellow socialists, the Marxists,
got away with mass murder through creating
academic circles. This inspired the
intellectuals behind holocaust revisionism to
create their own "think tanks" that lied as
wickedly as the Left.

Numerous people with university degrees
have joined the holocaust revisionist
movement in hopes of covering up the crimes
of National Socialism. These people are no
better than the liberals. It's monstrous to
hide the evil of your friends and comrades.

Why Nazism and White Racism Suck

When you do this, you are no better than the people who committed the murders. In truth, you become much worse because your true goal of covering up the past is so these crimes can happen again in the future. Be truthful, racist intellectual, you and your evil twin brother, the Left, uses academia to cover up the past in order to repeat your crimes again and again.

Stay out of holocaust revisionism. If you don't, you will become just as corrupt as the liberals.

Chapter Four

There is a Better Way

The racist movement and its Golden Child, National Socialism, suck greasy dog dicks.

They are a dead-end street. If you want to guarantee the White race will fail and become extinct, promote the racist movement and Neo-Nazism, which is why the Left wing builds up these nuts every chance they can. Do you really think that if the Left thought the racist movement would amount to anything ever that they would be giving it all the free publicity they are? They know that by promoting the shit out of the racist movement as "the only show in town" that they will quash any hopes of a White Reawakening. No sane person would ever join the racist movement, and most White people are sane. The racist movement isn't anything but a Cash Cow to the Left that they can march out, build up, and knock down any

Why Nazism and White Racism Suck

time they need funds from their donors.

If you hate the White race, join the racist movement. If you wish to empower the Left, put on a Nazi uniform and march up and down the street. The racist movement is pure poison. We can't base the survival of our people on hate.

Hate harms everyone, including the hater.

We must build our people on love for ourselves, our culture, our history, our community, and our heritage. Love can take us far. Hate will not.

Your hate just feeds the hate of those who hate the White race. What good do you do fueling the Left with your hate? It sure the fuck doesn't inspire White people. It empowers the enemies of the White race, which makes you, young racist, an even worse enemy of the White race than the Left.

If you really wish to help the White race, then get the fuck out of the racist movement altogether, get married, and start a large White family. This is what is needed. Have lots of babies and teach them the truth about our people and teach them to reject the defamation that democracy heaps on our

people. Fuck the system! It is the devil.
However, National Socialism or some other
system built upon racist hate is no better
than liberal democracy. All forms of
government suck. Your family is the only
thing of value. It's the only thing you can
trust. It will empower you and your progeny.
Build up your families. Create networks of
like-minded families. This is the future of
our people, not some government on the Left,
the Right, or the Center that centralizes
power in the hands of others. Family
government is power in your own hands. Isn't
that where power belongs? Fuck all these
totalitarian cults.

Our family, strong and proud, is the better
way.

Final Words

I purposefully made this booklet short. It is not written for people who are interested in attacking the White race. I wrote it for young people already in the movement or those thinking about joining. It will be a small miracle to get any of them to read a short criticism of "the movement" and impossible to get them to read a long one.

I have tons of criticism for racism, but these are a few points I think people in the movement or on the fringes will understand. Perhaps, I'll write more in the future, but this will do for now.

Hopefully, it will save young people from wasting a portion of their lives in hatesville.